Collins

Easy Learning

Times Tables

Age 5-7

My name is __Marriam__.

I am __five__ years old.

I go to __Broad Oak__ School.

My birthday is __15 May__.

**Simon Greaves
and Helen Greaves**

How to use this book

- Find a quiet, comfortable place to work, away from other distractions.

- Help with reading the instructions where necessary, and ensure that your child understands what they are required to do.

- Help and encourage your child to check their own answers as they complete each activity.

- Discuss with your child what they have learnt.

- Let your child return to their favourite pages once they have been completed, to talk about the activities.

- Reward your child with plenty of praise and encouragement.

Special features

- Yellow boxes: Introduce and outline the key times tables ideas.

- Did you know …? boxes: Give handy hints to help understanding of the key times tables ideas.

- Examples boxes: Show how to do the activity.

Published by Collins
An imprint of HarperCollins*Publishers*
77–85 Fulham Palace Road
Hammersmith
London
W6 8JB

Browse the complete Collins catalogue at www.collins.co.uk

© HarperCollins*Publishers* Limited 2006

10 9 8 7 6

ISBN-13 978-0-00-722260-5
ISBN-10 0-00-722260-2

The authors assert the moral right to be identified as the authors of this work.

All rights reserved. No part of this publication may be reproduced, stored in a retrieval system, or transmitted in any form or by any means, electronic, mechanical, photocopying, recording or otherwise, without the prior written permission of the Publisher or a licence permitting restricted copying in the United Kingdom issued by the Copyright Licensing Agency Ltd., 90 Tottenham Court Road, London W1T 4LP.

British Library Cataloguing in Publication Data
A Catalogue record for this publication is available from the British Library

Written by Simon Greaves and Helen Greaves
Design and layout by Graham M Brasnett
Illustrated by Jenny Tulip
Printed and bound in China

Contents

How to use this book	2
Two times table	4
Ten times table	8
Five times table	12
Mixed tables (twos, fives and tens)	16
Three times table	18
Four times table	22
Mixed tables (threes and fours)	26
Mixed tables (twos, threes, fours, fives and tens)	28
Answers	32

Two times table

The two times table tells you how to count in sets of two.

Read the two times table and count the sets.

1 × 2 = 2
2 × 2 = 4
3 × 2 = 6
4 × 2 = 8
5 × 2 = 10
6 × 2 = 12
7 × 2 = 14
8 × 2 = 16
9 × 2 = 18
10 × 2 = 20

Now fill in these answers.

2 × **1** = 2
2 × 2 = 4
2 × 3 = **6**
2 × **4** = 8
2 × 5 = 10
2 × 6 = **12**
2 × 7 = **14**
2 × 8 = 16
2 × **9** = 18
2 × **10** = 20

Did you know ... ?

All the answers in the two times table are **even** numbers.

An even number ends in **2**, **4**, **6**, or **8**.

Q1 The frog wants to get the fly. Colour a path with only the answers in the two times table.

Q2 Every number put into the number machine is **doubled**. Doubled means multiplied by **2**.

Fill in the missing numbers.

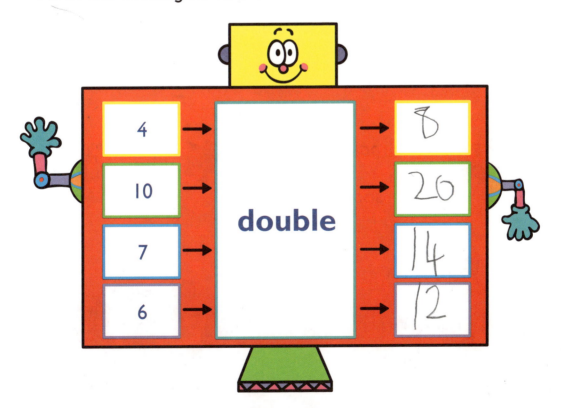

Q3 Count the coins and complete each multiplication.

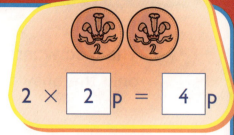

2 × 2 p = 4 p

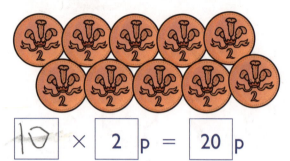

10 × 2 p = 20 p

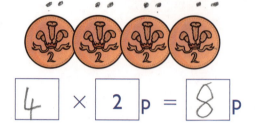

4 × 2 p = 8 p

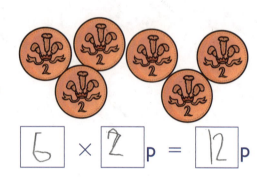

6 × 2 p = 12 p

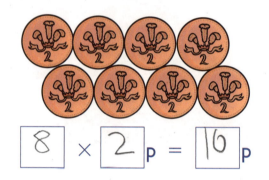

8 × 2 p = 16 p

Q4 Socks come in pairs. There are two socks in each pair.

For each picture write the number of pairs and socks.

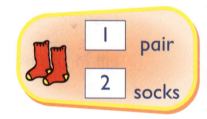

1 pair
2 socks

3 pairs
6 socks

5 pairs
10 socks

9 pairs
18 socks

7 pairs
14 socks

Q5 Draw a line to join each child to their matching kite.

Q6 If you roll two dice together you can get six different 'doubles'. You could get 1 and 1. This double scores 2.

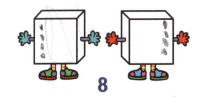

Draw dots on the dice to show doubles with these total scores.

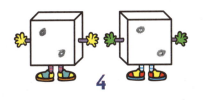
4

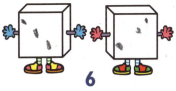
6

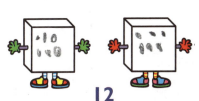
8

10   12

Ten times table

The ten times table tells you how to count in sets of ten.

Read the ten times table and count the sets.

1 × 10 = 10
2 × 10 = 20
3 × 10 = 30
4 × 10 = 40
5 × 10 = 50
6 × 10 = 60
7 × 10 = 70
8 × 10 = 80
9 × 10 = 90
10 × 10 = 100

Now fill in these answers.

10 × ☐ = 10
☐ × 2 = 20
10 × 3 = ☐
☐ × 4 = 40
10 × 5 = ☐
10 × ☐ = 60
☐ × 7 = 70
10 × ☐ = 80
10 × 9 = ☐
☐ × 10 = 100

Did you know ... ?

All the answers in the ten times table **end in zero**.

10, 20, 30, 40, 50, 60, 70, 80, 90, 100

Q1 Write a multiplication to show the total amount of money.

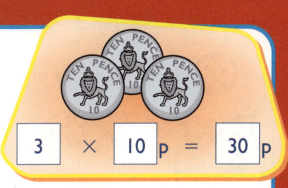

$3 \times 10\text{p} = 30\text{p}$

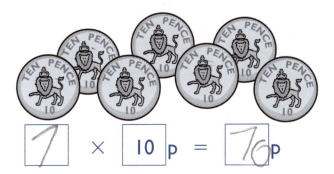

$7 \times 10\text{p} = 70\text{p}$

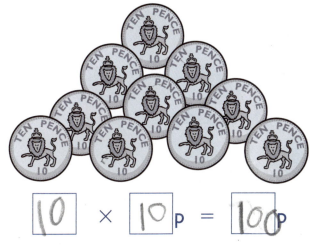

$10 \times 10\text{p} = 100\text{p}$

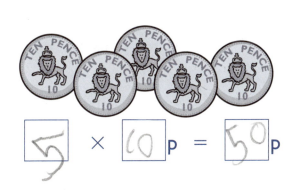

$5 \times 10\text{p} = 50\text{p}$

Q2 Colour green all the shapes that have an answer in the ten times table.

What do you see?

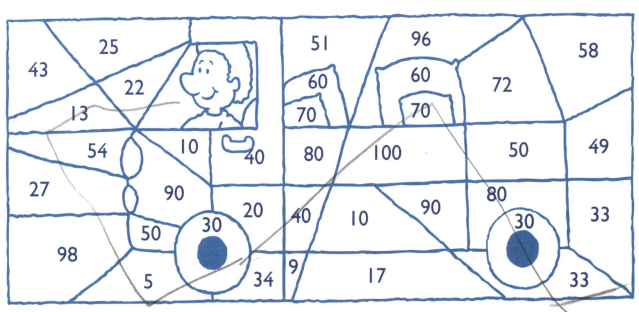

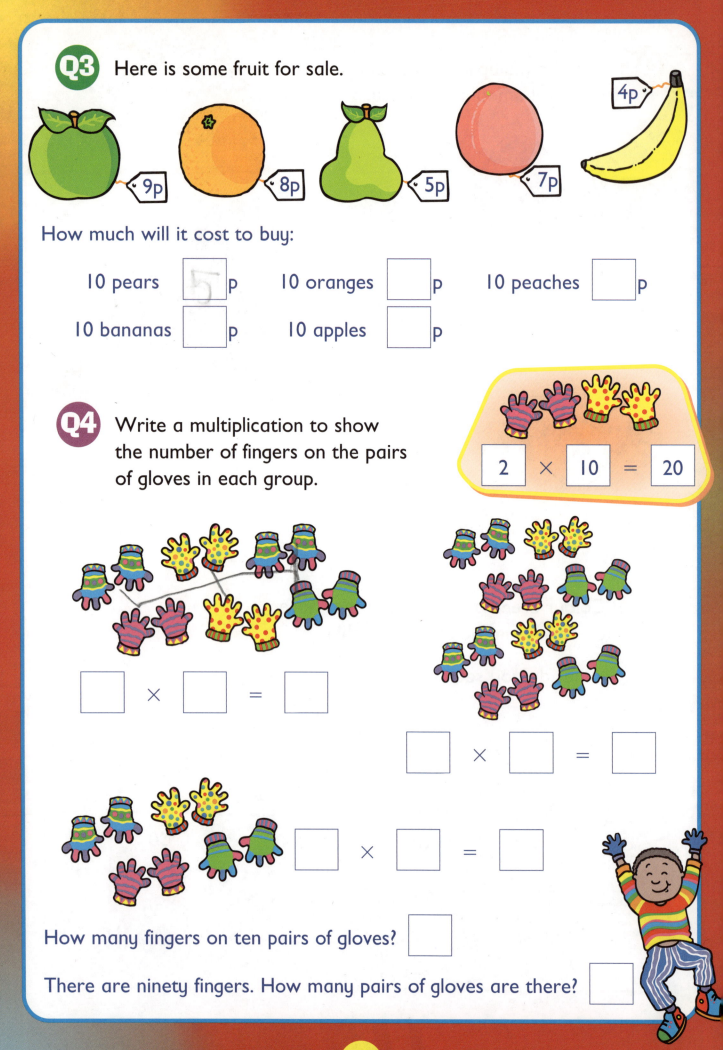

Q5 Every number put into the number machine is multiplied by 10. Fill in the missing numbers.

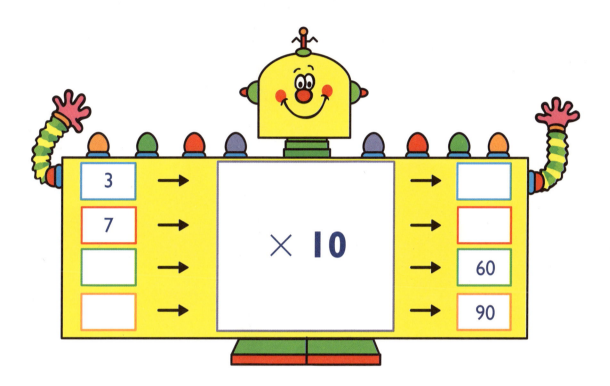

Q6 Say the multiples of ten as you join the dots. Join them in order. What do you see?

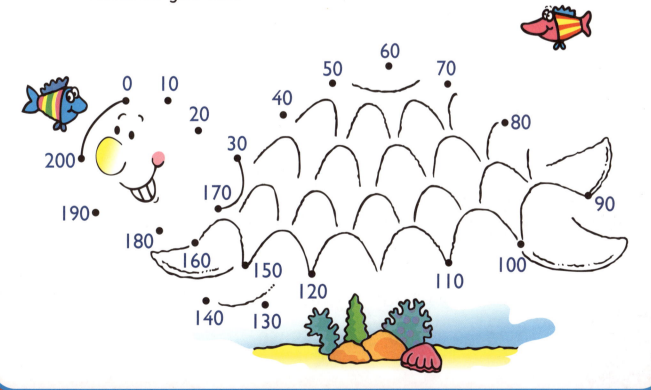

Five times table

The five times table tells you how to count in sets of five.

Read the five times table and count the sets.

1 × 5 = 5
2 × 5 = 10
3 × 5 = 15
4 × 5 = 20
5 × 5 = 25
6 × 5 = 30
7 × 5 = 35
8 × 5 = 40
9 × 5 = 45
10 × 5 = 50

Now fill in these answers.

☐ × 1 = 5
5 × 2 = ☐
5 × ☐ = 15
5 × 4 = ☐
5 × ☐ = 25
☐ × 6 = 30
5 × 7 = ☐
5 × 8 = ☐
☐ × 9 = 45
5 × ☐ = 50

Did you know ... ?

All the answers in the five times table end in **five** or **zero**.

5, 10, 15, 20, 25, 30, 35, 40, 45, 50

Q1 Complete these multiplications.

45 = 9 × 5

30 = ◯ × 5   5 = ◯ × 5   20 = ◯ × 5

50 = ◯ × 5   35 = ◯ × 5   10 = ◯ × 5

15 = ◯ × 5   25 = ◯ × 5   40 = ◯ × 5

Q2 Find the total in each purse.

2 × 5 p = 10 p

☐ × 5 p = ☐ p

☐ × ☐ p = ☐ p

☐ × ☐ p = ☐ p

Draw 5p pieces to show the amount next to each purse.

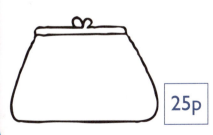 25p

 35p

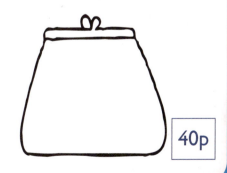 40p

Q3 Help the rabbit get the carrots. Fill in the missing numbers on the path.

After 50, count on in fives to 100.

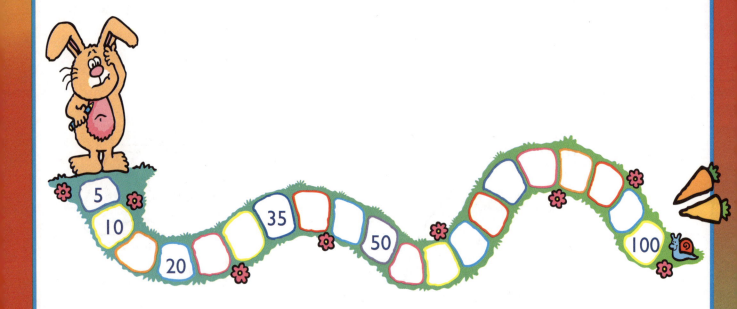

 Q4 The cat can only catch fish which are answers in the five times table.

Colour the fish he can catch.

Q5 In each line, circle the multiplication that matches the number in the star.

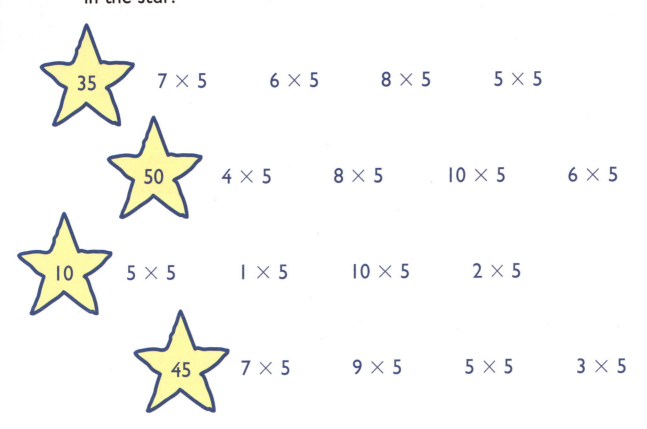

Q6 Work out the answer to each multiplication. Then use the answer to find the correct colour in the code key.

Colour the picture.

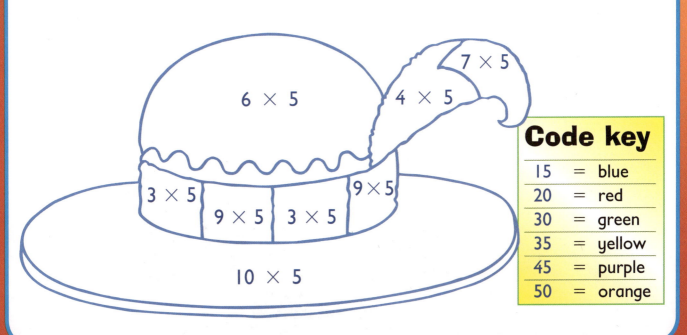

Code key

15	=	blue
20	=	red
30	=	green
35	=	yellow
45	=	purple
50	=	orange

Mixed tables

Did you know ... ?

When you multiply a number by two you can say that you are **doubling** it.

The opposite of **doubling** is **halving**.

Q1 Use the number machine to **double** each number.

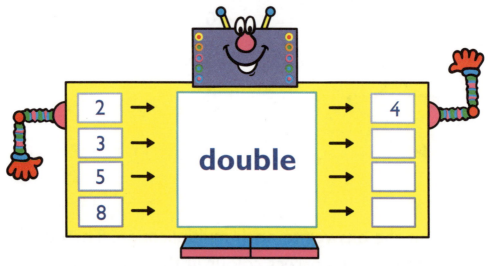

Use the number machine to **halve** each number.

Q2 10p can be made using 2p, 5p or 10p coins.

Make 20p using 2p, 5p or 10p coins.

Draw the coins in the purse and write the multiplication in the box below.

☐ × 2p = ☐ p   ☐ × 5p = ☐ p   ☐ × 10p = ☐ p

Q3 Work out the answer to each multiplication. Then use the answer to find the correct colour in the code key.

Colour the picture.

Code key
8	=	light blue
10	=	light green
15	=	dark blue
18	=	dark green
20	=	red
25	=	yellow

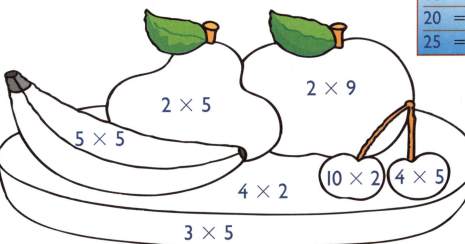

Three times table

The three times table tells you how to count in sets of three.

Read the three times table and count the sets.

1 × 3 = 3
2 × 3 = 6
3 × 3 = 9
4 × 3 = 12
5 × 3 = 15
6 × 3 = 18
7 × 3 = 21
8 × 3 = 24
9 × 3 = 27
10 × 3 = 30

Now fill in these answers.

☐ × 1 = 3
3 × ☐ = 6
3 × 3 = ☐
3 × ☐ = 12
3 × 5 = ☐
☐ × 6 = 18
3 × ☐ = 21
3 × 8 = ☐
☐ × 9 = 27
3 × ☐ = 30

Did you know ... ?

Every other answer in the three times table is an **odd** number.

An odd number ends in **1**, **3**, **5**, **7**, or **9**.

Q1 A tricycle has three wheels.

Write a multiplication to show the number of wheels on the tricycles.

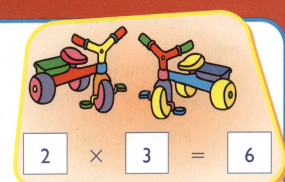

| 2 | × | 3 | = | 6 |

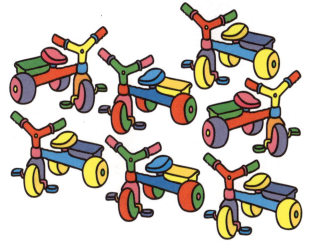

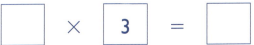 × 3 =

☐ × ☐ = ☐

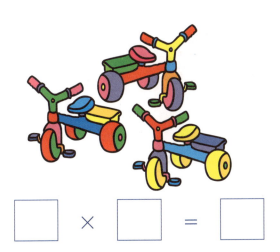

☐ × ☐ = ☐

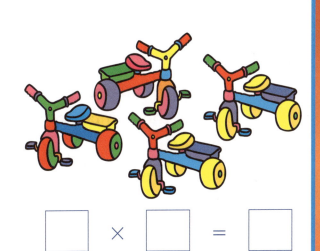

☐ × ☐ = ☐

Q2 Colour a path through the number grid.

Only go through answers to the three times table.

5	17	23	24	6	18	→ Finish
1	10	30	21	26	16
2	20	15	29	28	11
12	27	3	7	4	8
Start → 9	22	13	14	19	25

Q3 Each number that goes into the machine is multiplied by three.

Fill in the missing numbers.

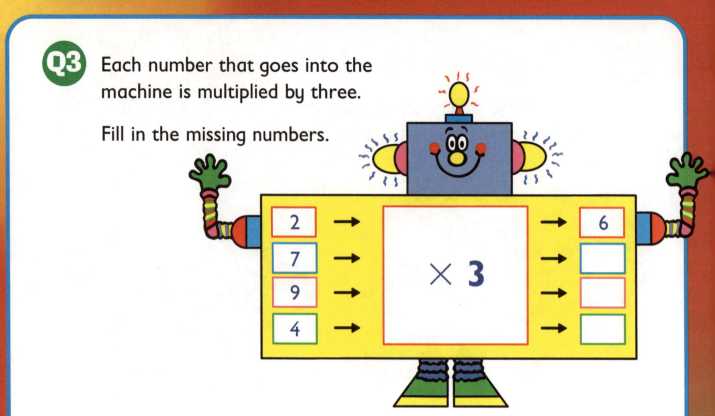

Q4 Colour each group of three sweets in a different colour.

Write a multiplication to show the number of sweets in each pile.

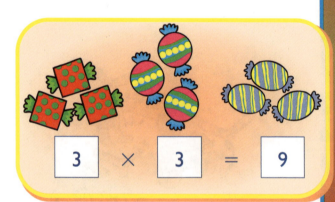

3 × 3 = 9

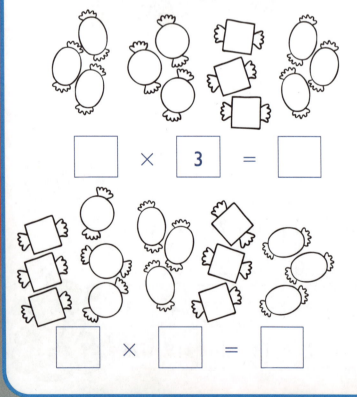

☐ × 3 = ☐

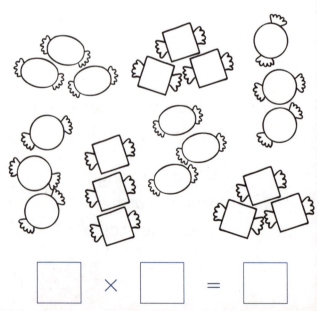

☐ × ☐ = ☐   ☐ × ☐ = ☐

Q5 These toys are for sale.

How much would it cost to buy:

3 yo-yos ☐ p　　3 crayons ☐ p　　3 bears ☐ p

3 pencil sharpeners ☐ p　　　　　　3 trains ☐ p

A pencil costs 3p.

How much would it cost to buy:

5 pencils ☐ p　　7 pencils ☐ p　　10 pencils ☐ p

Q6 Complete these multiplications using the three times table.

△ × 3 = 18　　　　△ × 3 = 24

△ × 3 = 12　　　　△ × 3 = 30

△ × 3 = 27　　　　△ × 3 = 3

△ × 3 = 6　　　　△ × 3 = 15

△ × 3 = 9　　　　△ × 3 = 21

Four times table

The four times table tells you how to count in sets of four.

Read the four times table and count the sets.

1 × 4 = 4
2 × 4 = 8
3 × 4 = 12
4 × 4 = 16
5 × 4 = 20
6 × 4 = 24
7 × 4 = 28
8 × 4 = 32
9 × 4 = 36
10 × 4 = 40

Now fill in these answers.

4 × ☐ = 4
4 × 2 = ☐
☐ × 3 = 12
4 × 4 = ☐
☐ × 5 = 20
4 × ☐ = 24
4 × 7 = ☐
4 × 8 = ☐
☐ × 9 = 36
4 × 10 = ☐

Did you know ... ?

Words linked to the number four have the letters 'qua' in them.

Like **square** and **quarter**!

Q1 There are four cakes in a box.

Write a multiplication to show the number of cakes altogether.

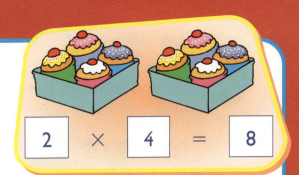

2 × 4 = 8

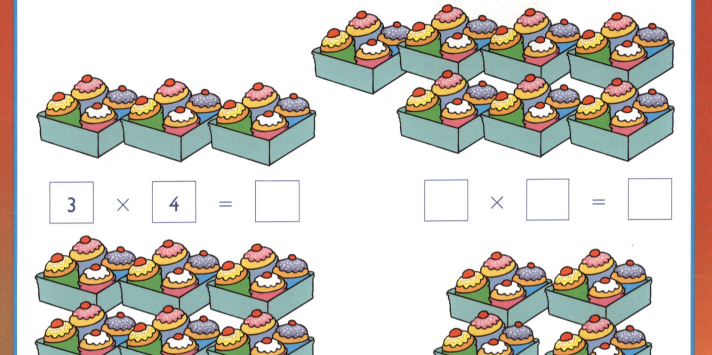

3 × 4 = ☐

☐ × ☐ = ☐

☐ × ☐ = ☐

☐ × ☐ = ☐

Q2 Every number put into the number machine is multiplied by 4.

Write in the missing numbers.

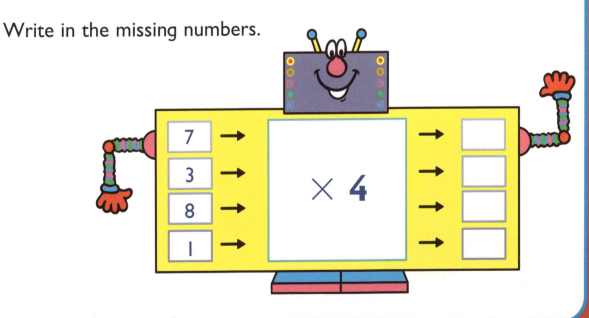

7 → × 4 → ☐
3 →   → ☐
8 →   → ☐
1 →   → ☐

Q3 Here are some things for sale.

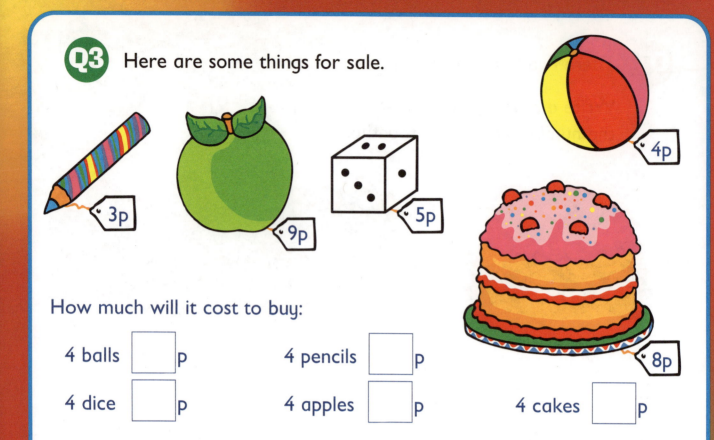

How much will it cost to buy:

4 balls ☐ p   4 pencils ☐ p

4 dice ☐ p   4 apples ☐ p   4 cakes ☐ p

Q4 Colour all the shapes that have an answer to the four times table.

What do you see?

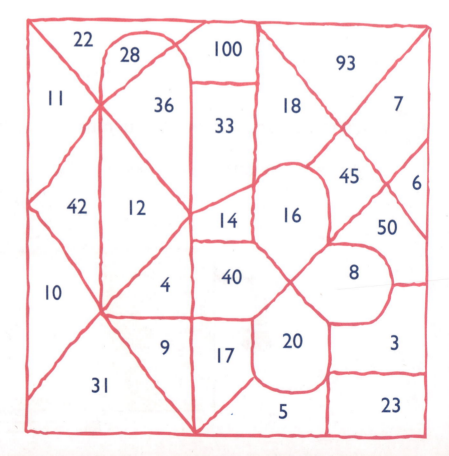

Q5 Here are the answers to the four times table.

Write in the missing numbers.

16 = ☐ × 4   28 = ☐ × 4

8 = ☐ × 4   20 = ☐ × 4

24 = ☐ × 4   40 = ☐ × 4

36 = ☐ × 4   4 = ☐ × 4

32 = ☐ × 4   12 = ☐ × 4

Q6 Some of the football players are wearing numbers which are answers to the four times table.

Circle the numbers.

Mixed tables

Did you know ... ?

The number 12 is an answer to the three and four times tables!

$$\begin{matrix} 3 \times 4 \\ 4 \times 3 \end{matrix} = 12$$

Q1 Count on in threes. Write the numbers on the orange snake.

Count on in fours. Write the numbers on the green snake.

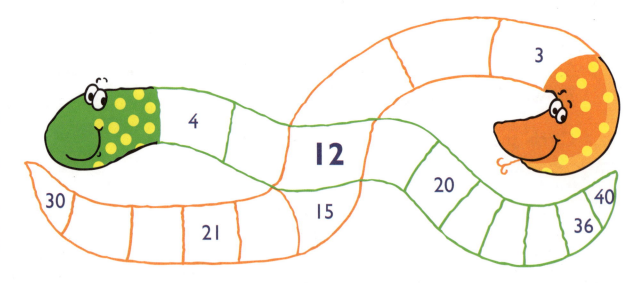

Q2 Draw a line to join each multiplication to its answer.

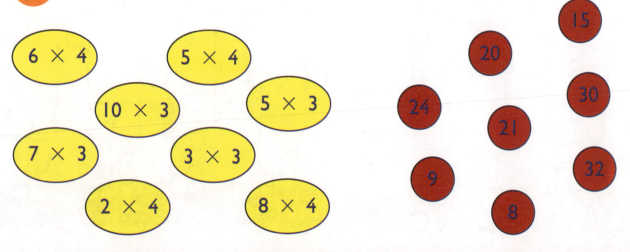

Q3 Here are some items for sale.

How much will it cost to buy:

3 rolls ☐ p   4 biscuits ☐ p   4 muffins ☐ p

3 cakes ☐ p   4 crumpets ☐ p   3 biscuits ☐ p

How many biscuits could you buy for 18p? ☐

How many crumpets could you buy for 24p? ☐

Q4 Answer these questions.

What are six threes? ☐   What is 2 times 4? ☐

What is 6 multiplied by three? ☐   Multiply 5 by 4. ☐

How many threes in 12? ☐   Divide 9 by 3. ☐

Which number multiplied by 3 is 18? ☐   How many fours in sixteen? ☐

Mixed tables

Q1 Write the missing number on each machine.

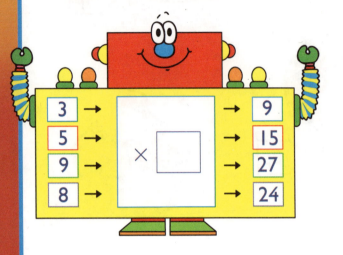
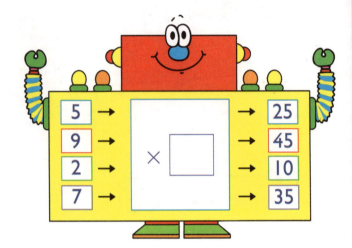
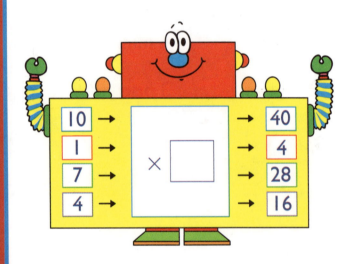
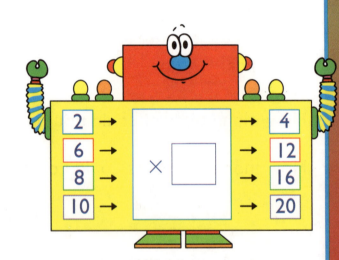

Q2 Draw lines to join the multiplications which have the same answer.

Q3 Look at these items.

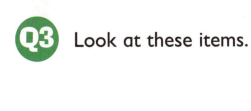

Answer these questions.

How many sweets in 7 jars? 7 × [10] = [70]

How many socks in 5 pairs? 5 × [ ] = [ ]

How many bananas in 6 bunches? 6 × [ ] = [ ]

How many cakes in 8 boxes? 8 × [ ] = [ ]

How many crayons in 3 packs? 3 × [ ] = [ ]

I have 16 cakes. How many boxes is this? [ ]

I have 40 sweets. How many jars is this? [ ]

I have 12 socks. How many pairs is this? [ ]

I have 20 crayons. How many packs is this? [ ]

I have 15 bananas. How many bunches is this? [ ]

Here are some multiplications. Some are right and some are wrong.

Tick those which have the right answer. Cross those which have the wrong answer.

4	×	5	=	20	✓	8	×	5	=	40
6	×	3	=	18		10	×	3	=	30
5	×	10	=	55		9	×	10	=	90
7	×	4	=	28		3	×	4	=	16

Did you know ... ?

 Look at the numbers below.

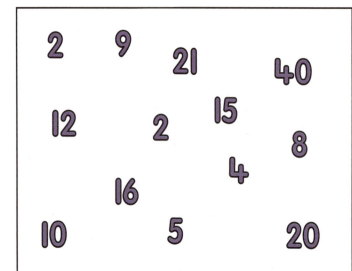

Some numbers are answers in more than just one times table!

Look at the answer 10. It is an answer in three different times tables!
1 × 10
2 × 5 = **10**
5 × 2

Circle any number which is in the two times table in blue.
Circle any number which is in the three times table in red.
Circle any number which is in the four times table in orange.
Circle any number which is in the five times table in green.
Circle any number which is in the ten times table in purple.

Have you noticed anything about these numbers?

Q6 Work out the answer to each multiplication. Then use the answer to find the correct colour in the code key.

Colour the picture.

Code key

10	=	dark blue
12	=	grey
20	=	green
30	=	yellow
40	=	light blue

 Q7 Answer these questions.

What is 7 times 3?

Multiply 6 by ten.

Which number mutliplied by 5 is 25?

How many threes in 24?

What are seven fours?

What is double 7?

Halve 18.

Divide 20 by 4.

Answers

Two times table

Page 4
1, 2, 6, 4, 2, 12, 14, 2, 9, 10

Page 5
Q1 10, 2, 20, 14, 12, 6, 18, 4, 16, 8
Q2 8, 20, 14, 12

Page 6
Q3 10 × 2p = 20p, 4 × 2p = 8p
6 × 2p = 12p, 8 × 2p = 16p
Q4 3 pairs and 6 socks, 5 pairs and 10 socks, 9 pairs and 18 socks, 7 pairs and 14 socks

Page 7
Q5 Join: 4 × 2 – 8, 9 × 2 – 18, 3 × 2 – 6, 6 × 2 – 12, 10 × 2 – 20, 7 × 2 – 14
Q6 4 – 2 dots on each dice
6 – three dots on each dice
8 – four dots on each dice
10 – five dots on each dice
12 – six dots on each dice

Ten times table

Page 8
1, 10, 30, 10, 50, 6, 10, 8, 90, 10

Page 9
Q1 7 × 10p = 70p
10 × 10p = 100p
5 × 10p = 50p
Q2 Colour the shapes numbered: 10, 20, 30, 40, 50, 60, 70, 80, 90, 100
It's a van!

Page 10
Q3 50, 80, 70, 40, 90
Q4 6 × 10 = 60, 8 × 10 = 80, 4 × 10 = 40
100, 90

Page 11
Q5 30, 70, 6, 9
Q6 Join the dots: 0–200 in the correct order.

Five times table

Page 12
5, 10, 3, 20, 5, 5, 35, 40, 5, 10

Page 13
Q1 30 = 6 × 5, 5 = 1 × 5,
20 = 4 × 5, 50 = 10 × 5,
35 = 7 × 5, 10 = 2 × 5,
15 = 3 × 5, 25 = 5 × 5,
40 = 8 × 5
Q2 3 × 5p = 15p, 4 × 5p = 20p,
6 × 5p = 30p
Check that your child has drawn: 5 × 5p, 7 × 5p, 8 × 5p

Page 14
Q3 15, 25, 30, 40, 45, 55, 60, 65, 70, 75, 80, 85, 90, 95
Q4 Colour fish: 5, 15, 45, 30, 35, 25

Page 15
Q5 Circle: 7 × 5, 10 × 5; 2 × 5, 9 × 5
Q6 6 × 5 – green, 4 × 5 – red,
7 × 5 – yellow, 3 × 5 – blue,
9 × 5 – purple, 10 × 5 – orange

Mixed tables

Page 16
Q1 Double: 6, 10, 16, Halve: 3, 5, 8

Page 17
Q2 10 × 2p = 20p, 4 × 5p = 20p,
2 × 10p = 20p
Q3 5 × 5 = yellow,
2 × 5 = light green,
2 × 9 = dark green,
4 × 2 = light blue, 10 × 2 = red,
4 × 5 = red, 3 × 5 = dark blue